The Flying Contest

An African story adapted by Ali Everts
Illustrated by Joe Morris

Characters

Narrator 4
Josh
Narrator 2
Narrator 1
Narrator 3
Narrator 5

Narrator 1: Are you sitting somewhere **comfortable**? We have a story to tell you.

Narrator 5: It's a **folk story**. If you know anything about folk stories, you'll know that they usually have a **moral**.

Josh: A moral? What's a moral? It sounds like a small furry animal.

Narrator 2: No, it's not a small furry animal. A moral is a little like a lesson.

Narrator 4: It's a message hidden in a story. It's a message that teaches you something.

Narrator 3: It's like the story of "The Three Little Pigs." That story has a lesson in it.

Josh: It does? Isn't it just a story about some silly little pigs that don't know how to build houses?

Narrator 5: Well, of course, that is the main point. But the moral is – as morals usually turn out to be – that hard work and good planning are the best ways to stay safe.

Narrator 1: Um, excuse me! Can we get on with telling the story now? It's an African folk story and it has a moral in it.

Josh: Sure, tell me the story. But how will I know which part is the moral?

Narrator 2: Listen carefully. See if you can figure it out.

Narrator 3: Okay, here we go. This folk story is called "The Flying Contest".

Josh: Does it have any small furry animals in it?

Narrator 4: Oh, please be quiet! It has nothing to do with small furry animals!

Narrator 5: One day, the birds of the air were arguing amongst themselves about which species could fly the highest. The big birds argued the most, especially Eagle.

Narrator 1: Nobody listened to the small birds. Nobody even looked at little Wren. She was one of the smallest birds of all.

Narrator 4: Nobody thought a small bird could fly high.

Narrator 2: To end the argument, the birds decided to have a contest. It would be in two weeks. They needed time to practise and make their wings strong.

Narrator 3: Wren spent the two weeks trying to think of a plan. She wanted to win, but she knew she couldn't fly as high as Eagle. He had the strongest wings of all.

Josh: Of course she couldn't win. No bird can fly higher than an eagle. I know what the moral is – don't take on anyone bigger than you are.

Narrator 4: Wait a minute! We need to finish. Now, where were we?

Narrator 5: Well, Wren, being a wise and thoughtful little bird, knew she would have to use her brain instead of her strength to win.

Narrator 1: The day of the contest finally came. All the birds flew into the air. They flew up and up, higher and higher.

Narrator 4: Wren flew as fast as she could. She tried to keep up with Eagle.

Narrator 2: One by one, the birds became tired and began to drop back. Then, as they reached the clouds, Wren landed softly on Eagle's back.

Narrator 3: Wren was as light as a feather. Eagle flew higher and higher. He laughed at the birds below him.

Narrator 4: "**Fools**!" Eagle shouted. "Did you really think you could win? Did you think you could beat me?"

Narrator 5: The birds below were all **cheering**. Eagle was certain that the roaring cheers were for him. He flew even faster, showing off how strong he was.

Narrator 1: Eagle didn't know that the other birds had seen Wren land on his back.

Narrator 4: The other birds were all cheering for Wren.

Narrator 2: "Who is flying the highest?" Eagle called as he flew above the clouds.

Narrator 3: "I am," said a little voice above him.

Narrator 4: Eagle was **amazed**. He flew even higher. Then he called again.

Narrator 5: "Who is flying the highest now?"

Narrator 1: "I am," said the little voice again.

Narrator 2: Eagle was angry. He flew higher and higher. He kept asking the same question.

Josh: Let me guess. Each time he asked, the little voice said, "I am."

Narrator 3: That's right. At last, Eagle was too tired to fly any more. He dropped slowly back to the ground. Before he did, Wren hopped off his back and flew even higher.

Narrator 2: Wren wasn't tired at all. She'd been riding on Eagle's back up to that point.

Narrator 4: She flew higher than everyone else, and all the birds cheered.

Narrator 5: And that, of course, brings us to the end of our tale.

Josh: What? Is that it? So, what's the moral?

Narrator 1: The moral of the story is that brains can be better than strength.

Josh: Oh. That's kind of what I was thinking. But maybe the moral actually goes something like this – small furry animals can be smarter than we think!

Narrators 1 to 5:
Argh!